This book is dedicated to Aline and William "Bras De Fer"

The author of this book Benjamin James Baillie lives and works in Normandy

Into the

Dragon's Lair

The Norman Conquest of Wales and the Marches

1066-1283

By
Benjamin James Baillie

Contents

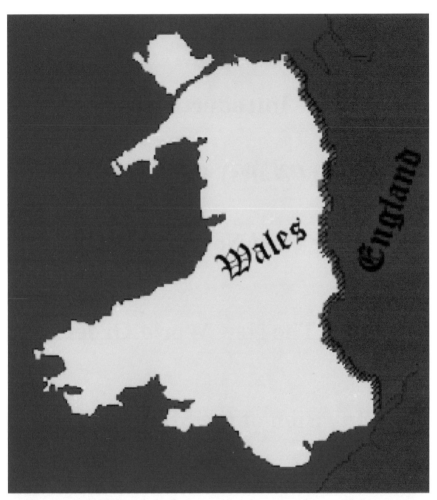

Map of Wales and the frontier 1066 ad

Celtic Wales

Norman England

Offas Dyke

Introduction

Wales was the first of the Celtic Kingdoms of the British Isles to face the Norman assault and invasion. Following the downfall of Anglo-Saxon England, William the Conqueror secured the frontier with Wales by establishing the Marcher Earldoms of Chester, Hereford and Shrewsbury. By 1088 the reins of the hated Norman Marcher lords had been effectively cut, allowing them to spearhead the conquest of Wales, which would take 200 years. The Welsh heirs of King Arthur were up against a cruel and cunning enemy, intent on destroying their way of life, identity and culture. The final showdown and reckoning would take place at the end of the 13th century when England's most ruthless warrior King Edward I invaded Wales.

Cymru (Wales) 410 – 1066 A.D

In the fifth century A.D the last Roman troops left Britain to defend the frontiers of the crumbling empire. The Island now entered the period of history known as the "Dark Ages".

The departure of the regular Roman field armies left Britannia virtually defenceless. In the north, the Picts overran Hadrian's Wall and raided the fertile lands of the south as far as London. Scottish tribes from Ireland also attacked the province from the west.

Germanic Dark age carving

By the middle of the century the Britons made a final appeal to Rome for assistance, in the form of a letter that became known as the "Groan of the Britons".

Gildas wrote:

"The barbarians drive us to the sea; the sea drives us to the barbarians; between these two methods of death we are either massacred or drowned"

Their pleas fell on deaf ears, as Rome was in no position to send troops or resources to help the Britons. The Romano-British leadership divided Britannia into three sectors; "Dux Britanniarum" commanded northern Britain from York and the remaining garrisons of Hadrian's Wall, "Comes Litoris Saxonici" commanded the south and the Saxon shore forts, and a mobile field army was placed under the command of the "Comes Britanniarum".

The Britons used the Roman tactic of recruiting barbarians to fight barbarians.
They employed Saxon mercenaries to help them defeat the Picts and Scots, but the newcomers realising the weakness of their paymasters revolted after the victory.

The White Horse Stone, The believed burial Place of the Saxon leader, Horsa

The Saxon Warlords, Hengest and Horsa, defeated the British high King Vortigern and the Britons in two pitched battles. Although Horsa was killed, the Anglo-Saxons had established a foothold on the Island.

King Arthur and the British fight back

The Germanic Angles, Saxons and Jutes slowly subjugated and pushed the native Romano-Britons west towards Wales and the western fringes of the country. The early Brythonic (British) Kingdoms of Powys, Gwynedd, Caerwent/Gwent, Dyfed and Brycheiniog emerged from the collapse of Roman Britain.

Between 490 and 550 A.D the shadowy hero figure of Celtic Britain, King Arthur halted the invaders. The real King Arthur was certainly part of the remaining Romano-British aristocracy. He may even have been Owain Ddantgwyn, the 5th century warlord of Powys. Owain's nickname was the bear (Arth / Arthur is also the Welsh name for the bear). His father also had the name "the terrible Dragon's head, which translates into Welsh as "Uthr Pen Dragon", King Arthur's father.

The Roman ruins of Wroxeter (capital of the Romano-British Kingdom of Powys)

According to the Welsh monk, Nennius, Arthur defeated the invaders in twelve battles. If this is true, Arthur may have been in command of a Roman/Sarmatian style cavalry cohort enabling him to cover the long distances to surprise and defeat the Germanic invaders who fought mainly on foot. At the Battle of "Mons Badonicus" the invaders were decisively defeated.

The Principality of Wales

Arthur had checked the invaders advance, but by the late 6th century the Saxons were on the move westward again. The Anglo-Saxons referred to the Britons as Welisc, (Welsh) from a Germanic word meaning 'foreigner'.
As they pushed into the modern day border area with Wales, resistance stiffened. King Offa of Mercia decided to define the border by constructing a mighty fortified earthwork known as Offa's Dyke. This Dyke defined the geographical area of the Principality of Celtic Wales. During the 9th ad 10th centuries the increased Viking attacks on England curtailed any Saxon ambitions on the Welsh, and eased the pressure on her eastern border with Mercia.

Offa's Dyke near Clun

From time to time a Welsh Prince or warlord would assert his power and authority over the other dominions within the Principality, such as Rhodri the Great and Hywel the Good, but any cohesion would vanish as soon as he died. Welsh law also hindered the forming of any long term power blocks and centralisation. When a Prince or family head died, the land was divided into equal shares between his sons.

The First Normans 1051

The first Normans to arrive on the Welsh border did not come with William the Conqueror in 1066. Some 15 years earlier, in 1051, King Edward the Confessor established a Norman colony in Herefordshire to defend the frontier against the Welsh. Ralph De Mantes became the first pre-conquest Norman Earl of Hereford.

He and a small band of Norman adventurers built the first Motte and Bailey castles in Britain. The English and Welsh had never seen anything like it before. The strange timber framed constructions were built on the huge earth worked Motte. Five castles were built, including Burghill and Richard's Castle near Ludlow.

The remains of Ewyas Harold Castle (Pre-Conquest Norman castle)

The Anglo-Saxon chronicle comments that:

"In September 1051, the French had built a castle"

In 1052 Norman and Celtic cultures clashed for the first time. The Welsh Prince, Gruffydd ap Llywelyn had successfully united most of Wales under his rule. He turned his attention towards raiding the English countryside. The Welsh advanced into Herefordshire and near Leominster they joined battle against a hastily unprepared force of Englishmen and Normans. The Welsh warriors using their spears and longbows decimated and put flight to the Anglo-Norman force. It was first blood to the Welsh, who returned with their booty back over the border.

In the following year, Gruffydd inflicted a second defeat upon the Anglo-Normans in Herefordshire. According to the Anglo-Saxon chronicle, the Anglo-Norman knights led by Ralph De Mantes were routed before the battle commenced.

The medieval city of Hereford

The Welsh then sacked and burned Hereford to the ground. The situation became so serious that Ralph was relieved of his command and replaced with Earl Harold Godwinson (the future King of England). In a series of devastating campaigns Harold defeated Gruffrydd and forced him to retreat into the mountains of Snowdonia. In 1063 the Prince of Wales met his end; Gruffrydd's own men murdered him, his head was cut off and sent to Harold as an act of submission.

1066 The New World Order

The Welsh feared the coming of the Normans in 1066. The foreign invaders had systematically destroyed Anglo-Saxon England within five years after the Battle of Hastings with ruthless efficiency. Although King William inherited the overlordship of Wales from his Anglo-Saxon predecessors, he probably never realistically contemplated the conquest of Wales.

William entrusted the defence of the Welsh border to his close companions, Hugh of Avranches, Earl of Chester, Roger Montgomery, Earl of Shrewsbury and William Fitz Osbern, Earl of Hereford. The first lords of the March had been given considerable freedom to enforce Norman control over the borderlands.

William Fitz Osbern constructed a network of defences along the southern Marches of Wales. He built Norman castles at Monmouth, Clifford and Wigmore to protect the approaches from Wales. His masterpiece was the construction of the mighty castle of Chepstow. It was one of the first stone built castles in Britain.

Chepstow castle, strategically positioned on the river Wye

The First Incursions

The ancient Celtic Kingdom of Caerwent/Gwent was the first region to fall to the Normans under William Fitz Osbern. The Norman war machine that entered Wales was very much different to the Anglo-Norman force that had been utterly beaten by the Welsh in 1052. The private army of Earl William routed the combined Welsh forces of Cadwgan ap Meurig and Maredudd Ab Owain (King of Deheubarth).

It was a shattering defeat for the Celtic warriors who were up against the chain clad armoured knights, who used the new tactics of combining infantry, cavalry and archers.

The Royal policy worked well, as long as loyal lieutenants controlled the frontier, but after the death of Fitz Osbern in 1071 the Earldom passed to his son Roger who rebelled against the King in 1075 (the revolt of the Earls).

The Norman Knight (Bayeux Tapestry)

This revolt altered King William's border strategy. In 1081 William paid a visit to St David's Church in Southwestern Wales. There he accepted the homage of Prince Rhys ap Tewdwr. This was an important development, for William hoped by promoting Rhys he could counter balance the power of the Marcher Lords.

By playing one side off against the other, neither one could become too powerful. The Norman raids into Wales ceased, but when William the Conqueror died in 1087 his iron fist was removed from the sensitive border area.

The Invasion of the Marcher Lords

The new King of England William II "Rufus" tried to continue the same policy of his father, but when a baronial revolt broke out in 1088 he was forced to offer concessions towards the Marcher lords. In return for their support he gave them a free hand to carve out an empire for themselves in the buffer states of Wales. Although they were restricted from directly attacking Rhys ap Tewdwr's Kingdom of Deheubarth, the adjoining state of Brycheiniog was classed as fair game.

Rhys ap Tewdwr came to the assistance of Bleddyn ap Maenarch, the beleaguered Lord of Brycheiniog. Together they marched out of the hills and confronted Bernard De Neufmarche who was constructing a castle near Brecon. The Welsh charged uphill against the Normans, but were cut to pieces by the mounted Norman knights. Rhys was killed in the vicious fighting and with him died the agreement made with King William.

The Normans crossed the border and overran most of Wales. In the north, Hugh de Avranches and his deputy Robert De Rhuddlan advanced up the Dee valley and captured Gwynedd and the Island of Anglesey. Roger De Montgomery was responsible for the massive territorial gains in the middle March and in south Wales; His armies wiped out Welsh resistance in the south, Pembrokeshire and Glamogan became so populated with Normans and English that the Welsh tongue virtually disappeared. Pembrokeshire became known and still is to this day called "little England beyond Wales".

Overleaf the death of Rhys ap Tewdwr at Brecon →

Pembroke Castle, Wales

The Prince of Gwynedd

The invasion lost its momentum when Earl Roger died in 1094. The Welsh on the other hand gained a figurehead in the form of Gruffydd ap Cynan. Gruffydd, "Prince of Gwynedd", had languished in the rotting prison cells of the hated Norman Marcher Lord Hugh De Avranches "Hugh the Wolf" for over 10 years.

One day in 1094 a Welsh merchant by the name of Cynwric spotted the Prince of Gwynedd enchained outside the newly Norman built castle in Chester. The once proud man had been reduced to an object of derision. The crowd gathered around him, jeering and insulting him. In the evening Cynwric plied the guards with liquor and set the Prince free.

Like the Scottish hero Braveheart, Gruffrydd championed the fight back against the Norman invaders. The rebellion spread rapidly and within a year all of Wales was in revolt. The Normans could scarcely leave the safety of their castles for fear of being ambushed.

Gruffrydd's guerilla war helped the Welsh regain much of Wales lost to the Normans. He chose to avoid pitched battles where the Normans could use their superior tactics and cavalry. Instead he attacked them in the woodland and mountainous terrain of the country.

The Normans were also forced to change their strategy; they started an intense construction of new castles. These castles were built in strategic positions, guarding the entrances to the Welsh uplands. The Normans sort to control the fertile valleys, leaving the Welsh in control of the pastoral uplands.

Return of the Vikings 1098

In 1098 the Normans chased Prince Gruffydd onto the Island of Anglesey. The Prince retreated and took safe passage to Ireland. Anglesey suffered the full fury of the Normans. The Holy church of Llandyfrydog was desecrated, and used as a kennel for the hunting dogs of the Earl of Shrewsbury. Even the clergy was not exempt from retribution: an elderly priest was mutilated and anyone believed to be a rebel was executed on the spot.

The Normans were surprised by a Viking raiding fleet of King Magnus of Norway. The dragon-head ships arrived off the Coast of Puffin Island. In the battle that ensued, the two armies fought each other to a standstill, but the Normans retreated when Earl Hugh De Montgomery was shot and killed by a stray Viking arrow.

Gwenllian, The Warrior Princess

In the south, the Welsh were led by Gwenllian, the daughter of Gruffydd. This brave warrior Princess resisted the Normans with a burning hatred. The end came when she was betrayed by a fellow countryman, to the Marcher Lord, Maurice de Londres. Near Kidwelly Castle she made a last desperate stand against overwhelming odds. She fought gallantly with sword in hand until she was finally overwhelmed and taken prisoner. Gwenllian and her surviving son were both decapitated after the battle on the orders of Maurice De Londres. The battle site is still called Gwenllian's field. Legend has it that it took its name because Gwenllian's severed head never left the field. Gwenllian's death only encouraged others to rise up against the Normans. At the battle of Llwcher they ambushed and defeated a Norman force commanded by Richard Fitz Gilbert

The Norman castle of Kidwelly near Gwenllian's last stand

Owain Gwynedd

Gwenllian's brothers, Owain Gwynedd and Cadwaladr, continued the rebellion against the Normans. They defeated them at the battle of Llwchwr and won a resounding victory just outside Cardigan at the Battle of Crug Mawr. The Normans were slaughtered in the bloody conflict, and are reported to have lost 3000 men. In the rout that followed the battle, they attempted to cross a wooden bridge over the river Teifi. The bridge collapsed into the river because of the sheer weight of soldiers trying to cross it. Many of the Norman knights and foot soldiers fell into the cold river and drowned.

Within 20 years Owain was the master of most of Wales. His victories caught the attention of Henry Plantagenet, King of England and the most powerful monarch in Europe, with an Empire that stretched from the borders of Scotland to the Spanish frontier.

Arms of Owain Gwynedd

The King invaded Wales to put Owain back in his place and restore the balance of power between the Welsh and the Marcher lords. The Royal army ravaged the towns and villages along the north Wales coastline, burning down churches and settlements as they went. The Welsh, who had become masters of guerrilla warfare, ambushed the Normans in a wooded valley at Ewloe. As the Norman advanced guard passed into the valley, the Welsh who were waiting, suddenly started running down the slopes shouting the cry "Maes Gwenllian" in honour of their brave warrior Princess.

Overleaf: Henry D'Essex losing the royal banner to the Welsh→

Unable to use their heavy cavalry in the narrow gorge, the Normans were annihilated. As the fog descended from the hills above, a massacre followed. In the melec, the King only just avoided capture. His standard bearer, Henry D'Essex lost the royal banner to the Welsh. It was a catastrophic defeat for the proud Normans.

The Battle of Crogen 1165 A.D

Not deterred by the defeat, Henry returned again to Wales in 1165. He entered the interior of Wales to try and bring Owain to battle. In the dense wooded Ceiriog valley beneath the Berwyn mountains, disaster stuck again. The Norman foresters cut down the trees making way for Henry's massive army. The clouds darkened and the rain lashed down on the Royal army, and then at Bron-y-garth Owain's men ambushed the Normans.

They came out of the mist, hurling spears and using the deadly Welsh longbow to devastating effect. Henry was nearly killed, and was only saved by the bravery of Hugh De Saint Clare, who flung himself between the King and the Welsh tribesmen, being killed in the process.

Plaque commenerating the Battle of Crogen 1165 A.D

Many men were killed in the vicous hand to hand combat of the forest battlefield. Henry retreated, but in a callous act of vengeance, he ordered the eyes of Owain's two sons, who were his hostages, to be torn out.

The Marcher Lords

Today the Welsh Marches are essentially the border areas with England, but in the middle ages over half of the present day Wales was a Marcher lordship.

The Marcher lords ruled their newly conquered lands in Wales as they saw fit. In England they were subject to the King's law, but in the Marches they could build a castle without licence, raise private armies and had the right to exercise justice according to the law and customs of the March.

Indeed each lordship had its own different customs, a mixture of Welsh and English law. When a Royal messenger arrived in the Marcher lordship of Walter De Clifford, he was forced to eat the Royal writ, parchment and even the wax seal.

Another infamous Marcher lord was William De Braose: the De Braose name became a byword for treachery in Wales.

When Milo Fitz Walter was killed by the native Welsh in 1175, his lands passed in the hands of his nephew William De Braose.

Arms of William de Braose

The Massacre of Abergavenny

William determined to avenge the death of his uncle, invited all the local Welsh chiefs and leaders to his castle at Abergavenny for the Christmas celebrations.

As the Welsh nobility were feasting, William gave the signal to his Norman guards who went to work and murdered the Welsh in cold blood.

The bloody events of that night became known as the "Massacre of Abergavenny". William even hunted down the seven year old son of Seisyll ap Dyfnwal (the Welsh lord of upper Gwent) and had him put to death. For these evil deeds the Welsh nicknamed him the "Ogre of Abergavenny". The massacre of Abergavenny was not an isolated event, another Welsh Prince called Trahaiarn was dragged through the streets of Brecon, tied to the tail of a horse, before being beheaded on the orders of William De Braose in the town's market square.

The Welsh Avengers

The Welsh never forgot the cruel treatment of De Braose. On several occasions they tried to kill the Marcher Lord and his henchmen. In a nighttime raid they gained access to Abergavenny Castle. The garrison was murdered and the castle was burned to the ground.

Ranulf Poer (the sheriff of Herefordshire) who had actually committed some of the murders of the Welsh tribesmen and women after the massacre of Aberganenny, met his end at the hands of the vengeful Welsh in 1182. The Celtic warriors stormed the unfinished walls of the newly built stone castle of Dingestow in Monmouthshire. The Norman guards were overwhelmed and Ranulf was beheaded for his evil crimes against the native population. William De Braose escaped justice and survived all the attempts against his life. After an ambush by the Welsh, he was found hiding in a ditch. They dragged him out, but he was saved at the last minute by his bodyguard of mounted knights.

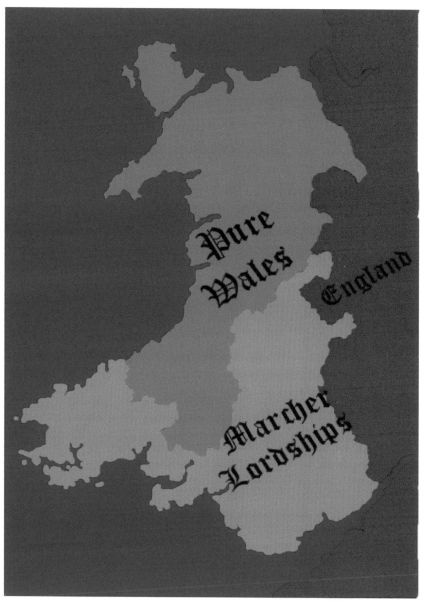

Map of Wales and the Marches 1250 A.D

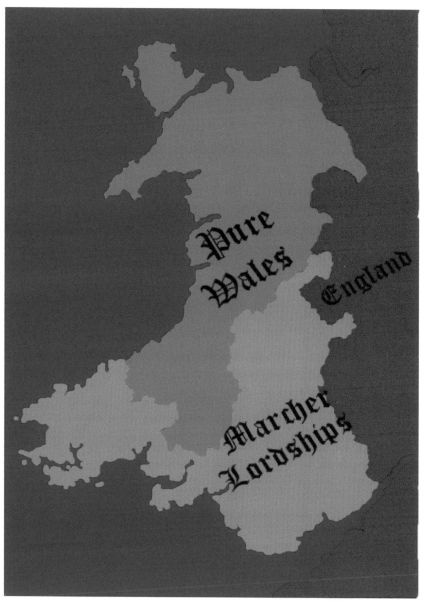 England

 Pure / Celtic Wales

 The Marcher Lordships

The De Mortimers "Earls of March"

One of the most famous and powerful families on the March was the House of Mortimer. The De Mortimers came from a small village in Normandy, France, called Mortemer sur Elaune. Even today the remains of their Motte and Bailly castle can still be seen. Ralph De Mortemer came over with William the Conqueror and was closely related to Earl Roger De Montgomery and William Fitz Osbern. It is possible that Ralph de Mortemer was part of William Fitz Osbern's retinue during the campaign against Edric the wild in 1067-1069. The Wigmore chronicle states that Ralph captured Edric

"After a long struggle Edric was captured and handed over to the King for life imprisonment, afterwards some of his lands became part of the abbey of Wigmore."

By 1086 Ralph was the established lord of the small village of Wigmore on the border with Wales

The Domesday book records;

The Mortimer arms

"Ralph de Mortemer holds WIGEMORE castle. Earl William built it on wasteland which is called MERESTUN, which Gunfrid held before 1066. Ralph has 2 ploughs in lordship and 2 hides which pay tax, and 4 slaves. The Borough which is there pays £ 7."

Slowly but surely the Mortimers rose in power from their family seat of Wigmore castle. Like the De Braoses they were ruthless in their attitudes towards the native Welsh.

They had no compulsion in committing acts of great cruelty. A Welsh chronicler wrote that when Prince Rhys ap Howel was captured by Hugh De Mortimer the late 1140s, his eyes were put out and he and his son were later put to death. The Mortimers would use any means necessary to gain control and enlarge their Marcher lands in Wales.

The ruins of Wigmore castle, (The Mortimer family seat and powerbase for over 200 years)

In 1179 Hugh II was implicated in another treacherous act: Prince Cadwallon ap Magog was murdered whilst travelling in the March under the safe conduct of the King.

Ludlow castle, Shropshire, acquired by the De Mortimer family at the end of the 13th Century

Llywelyn Fawr (the Great)

Llywelyn Fawr followed in the footsteps of his great grandfather (Owain Gwynedd) and led the resurgence against the Normans. Ironically he modeled himself on Henry Plantagenet, King of England, and united all of Pure Wales under his just rule.

He was probably born at Dolwyddelan castle, in the heart of Snowdonia in 1173. By 1200 he was the undisputed Prince of Gwynedd.

He further consolidated his power by annexing Eifionydd and Llyn.

Statue of Liywelyn Fawr, Conway

In 1201 his territorial gains were recognised by King John in return for Llywelyn's oath of fealty and vassalage. He married Joan Plantagenet (the illegitimate daughter of King John) in 1205, thus strengthening the ties with England. When Gwenwynwyn of Powys fell foul of the King in 1208, Llywelyn invaded southern Powys and occupied his lands. In 1209 he was summoned by his overlord King John, and accompanied the King in a campaign to overawe the Scots.

The following year Prince Llywelyn fell from grace, and his relationship with the King deteriorated. His alliance with the infamous De Braose family may have contributed to this factor, or it may just have been that the King thought Llywelyn was becoming too big for his boots and decided to check the Prince's power.

Dolwyddelan castle, Snowdonia, Llywelyn's possible birthplace

The first campaign led by the Earl of Chester ended in failure. Llywelyn used the same guerrilla tactics as his grandfather and forced the Normans to retreat back to England. The King decided to lead the army himself and invaded Wales in the summer of 1211. Gwynedd was devastated by the Normans, and Banger was burned to the ground. Prince Llywelyn had no choice but to come to the

King and submit. He was forced to accept the harsh terms: all the land east of the river Conway (known as the four Cantrefs) was to be surrendered, and the Prince was heavily fined for his disloyalty. Only the pleading of his wife Joan to her father allowed Llywelyn to keep his title and the remaining territory of Gwynedd.

The Recovery

Prince Llywelyn was able to take full advantage of the baron's growing dispute with King John. By 1216 he had recovered the Four Cantrefs and had united most of Wales under his banner.

In March 1218, the treaty of Worcester was concluded between the new King Henry III and Prince Llywelyn. In return for his homage to Henry, Llywelyn's recent conquests were ratified by the King.

The Prince's power now started to encroach on the great Marcher family of

Arms of Llywelyn the Great

the Marshals, who dominated South Wales. Sir William Marshall was the most respected and feared knight of the age. He had served some of the most powerful monarchs in Europe, Henry Plantagenet, Eleanor D'Aquitaine, Richard the Lionheart, King John and Henry III. In 1190, he had married Isabelle De Clare (the daughter of the Norman Conqueror of Ireland, Strongbow/Richard de Clare). This marriage made him the most extensive Norman landowner in south Wales.

Prince Llywelyn did not attack the lands of the old warrior until after his death in 1219. While the new Earl of Pembroke (William Marshal the younger) was restoring Norman rule in Ireland, Llywelyn seized his chance and invaded the Marshal lordships, capturing the important castles of Carmarthen and Cardigan. In the spring of 1224, William Marshal returned from Ireland and re-captured most of the territory lost in the previous year.

Under the influence of the Prince, a series of Welsh castles were refortified and constructed at Castell y Bere, Criccieth, Dolbadarn and Dolwyddelan, defending Wales against the Norman threat. The tit for tat warfare continued in Wales for the rest of the Prince's reign. Both sides would gain the upper hand before castles and prisoners were exchanged in the treaties that followed.

Sarcophagus of Llywelyn the Great, St Grwst Church, Llanrwst.

In 1234 "the peace of Middle" treaty established an uneasy truce between the Normans and the Welsh. In 1240 at the age of 68 Llwelyn "Prince of north Wales and Lord of Snowdonia" died peacefully leaving the Principality of Wales stronger than it had been in a generation.

Dafydd and Gruffudd

Dafydd succeeded his father as Prince of Gwynedd in spite of the fact that he had an older brother Gruffudd. Gruffudd had been excluded from his inheritance because he was anti-English and his father knew that if Gruffudd succeeded him, it would have meant continued warfare with England, which in the long run the Welsh could not hope to win. Dafydd on the other hand had married Isabella De Braose and with this union Llywelyn hoped that the ties with England would strengthen the position of a semi-independent Wales.

The majestic setting of Criccieth castle, North Wales

When Dafydd became Prince, he imprisoned his brother Gruffudd. He was kept prisoner under close guard in the newly built Welsh castle of Criccieth. The situation with King Henry III deteriorated over the lands outside Gwynedd which both rulers claimed. In 1241 Henry III invaded Wales and forced Dafydd to sign the treaty of Gwerneigron.

Dafydd agreed to relinquish the "Four Cantrefs" and also hand over his brother Gruffudd, whom Henry III hoped to use as a puppet in England if Dafydd had any visions of grandeur.

The Tower of London 1244

After three years of English captivity in the Tower of London, Gruffudd could take no more and decided to make his escape. On St David's Day 1244 he made a makeshift rope ladder out of tapestries, and started the abseil down the walls of the mighty White Tower. Suddenly, the rope snapped and Gruffudd fell to his death. The force of the fall was so great that it is said his head was pushed between his shoulders.

Back in Wales Dafydd used the martyr-like death of his brother and rival, to galvanise the Welsh people

The death of Gruffud, 1244 A.D

and rid themselves of the Normans once and for all. Disillusioned with the way Henry had treated him, he decided to take the war to the Normans. The Welsh harried the lands of the "Four Cantrefs". Henry III retaliated and invaded Gwyenedd. The King was frustrated at being unable to bring Dafydd to battle, and ordered some Welsh prisoners who had been captured during a raid on a shipwrecked Irish supply boat, to be beheaded on the beach. Dafydd in turn executed the Normans he had captured in the campaign, and threw their bodies into the river Conwy.

Both armies retired with the onset of winter, preparing themselves for the decisive campaign due in 1246. Henry implemented an economic embargo on all trade between Wales and England, hoping to break the will of the Welsh people and force them to submit to their eastern neighbour.

The final showdown was not meant to be, as Dafydd died early in 1246 leaving Gwyenedd to be divided between his family members. He was buried alongside his father at the abbey of Aberconwy with the epitaph

'Tarian Cymru' - The shield of Wales

Llywelyn the Last

In 1246 Prince Dafydd died childless; he was succeeded by his nephew Llywelyn ap Gruffudd, the son of the unfortunate Gruffudd who fell to his death at the tower of London. Llywelyn and his brother Owain begrudgingly acknowledged King Henry III as their overlord and were forced to cede the disputed area of the "Four Cantrefs" to him at the treaty of Woodstock in 1247.

Llwelyn ap Gruffudd

The King intended to limit the powers of Llywelyn by breaking up the already small principality of Gwynedd. When Llywelyn's brother Dafydd came of age, the King in his office as overlord offered him some territory in Gwynedd. Llywelyn was outraged and refused to comply. In 1255 he went to war against his brothers and decisively beat them at the battle of Byrn Derwin.

As the undisputed Prince of Gwynedd, Llywelyn decided to take the offensive and free his fellow Welshmen and women who were being oppressed by the Normans in the "Four Cantrefs". The Perfeddwlad, as it was called, had been given by the King to his son Prince Edward Plantagenet. Edward had visited his fief in 1256 but had treated his Welsh subjects with contempt and had failed to address the grievances they had regarding the oppressive rule.

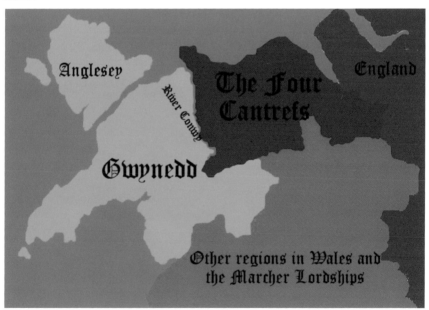

Map of North Wales

Disillusioned with their Norman lord, the Welsh begged Llywelyn for help. In the winter of 1256 he crossed the river Conwy and quickly overran the entire region. Only the castles of Deganwy and Dyserth held out. When the news reached the royal court in England, Prince Edward was furious and hell-bent on returning the Wales to punish Llywelyn.

Matthew Paris commented;

"Edward was determined to punish the Welsh and exterminate those who dared challenge his authority"

Winter storms forced Edward to abandon any hopes he had to recapturing the "Four Cantrefs". Llywelyn now master of most of north Wales turned south and took Powys, and then Deheubarth. All across Wales the people flocked to his banner and ousted the hated Marcher lords. The rising even reached the Norman stronghold of the Gower lordship, Kidwelly town was ransacked and burned to the ground. The Norman Castilian De Chatsworth was besieged in the castle, but managed to hold out.

Prince Edward Plantagenet

The Battle of Coed Llathen / Cadfan

A Norman counterattack led by Sir Stephan Bacon from Carmarthen was wiped out at the battle of Cadfan.

In the thick wooded and boggy terrain the Norman knights were ambushed and killed. Sir Stephan was pulled from his horse and hacked to pieces in the stream at Pentrefelin. A small bridge "Pont Steffan" was named after him. The disaster sent shockwaves back to England.

King Henry III was left with no choice but to lead the army with his son Prince Edward into Wales to put down the rebellion. From Chester the royal army advanced along the north Wales coastline as so many armies had done before it. They retook the "Four Cantrefs" and forced the Welsh back over the river Conwy, but with supplies running low the King abandoned the campaign and returned to England.

The failure of the campaign of 1257 left Llywelyn in an extremely favourable position. He once again crossed the river Conwy and re-occupied the "Four Cantrefs". While England was slipping into civil war between the King and the barons led by Simon De Montfort, Llywelyn extended his gains in Wales and the Marches. Another one of Prince Edward's castles, Builth was captured by Llywelyn's forces in 1260.

The Battle of Evesham 1265

Llywelyn even sent Welsh troops off to help Simon De Montfort in his struggle against the monarchy. On the 4th of August 1265 Simon and his Welsh allies were trapped at Evesham. When the royalist forces came into view Simon is reported to have said;

"May the Lord have mercy upon our souls, as our bodies are theirs"

The only escape route, the Bengeworth Bridge, had been captured by tenacious Marcher lord Roger De Mortimer. Simon De Montfort had no choice but to try and fight his way out against overwhelming numbers. Prince Edward who commanded the Royal forces ordered that no quarter would be given.

As the battle commenced, a thunder storm from the heavens above lashed rain and lightning down on the two opposing armies. Simon and his men fought valiantly: he hacked his way deep into the Royalist ranks, trying to force a way through. His son Henry spattered with blood and mud was cut down and put to death, then Roger De Mortimer charged straight at Simon and killed him with his lance. The brave warrior was set upon and mutilated beyond recognition, his head, hands, feet and testicles were cut off. Simon's head was sent back to Wigmore castle as a trophy of war by the victorious Roger De Mortimer. The unfortunate Welsh archers and infantry who survived were also executed, or forced into the services of the Marcher lords.

The aftermath of the battle of Evesham: Simon De Montfort being mutilated

The Marcher Lord
Roger De Mortimer at the Battle of Evesham
1265

The Treaty of Montgomery 1267

In 1267 King Henry and Prince Edward travelled to the Welsh border to broker a peace deal with the Welsh. The outcome of the treaty was a masterstroke for Llywelyn: he was officially acknowledged by Henry as the Prince of Wales. This was the first and only time an English King bestowed the title of Prince of Wales on a native Welshman. All the other Welsh nobles now gave homage to Llywelyn instead of Henry. The Four Cantrefs were surrendered including Prince Edward's castle of Builth. The Lordship of Brecon was also handed over to the Prince. It was the pinnacle of Llywelyn's career. He had achieved more than any other Welsh leader could have hoped for, the right to rule his country and people as an independent ruler.

The Poisoned Chalice

Llywelyn knelt before King Henry III and performed the ceremony of homage, ratifying the treaty. The only snag with the Treaty of Montgomery was that it came at a price: Llywelyn would have to pay over 20,000 marks for his title and the agreement, but his annual income was probably only about 5,000 marks a year in total.

The other problem was the Norman Marcher lords who controlled most of the fertile southern part of Wales.

Llywelyn's title would be his downfall, for he did not have enough money to pay the annual payments to the King and fund the re-organisation and defence of the Principality against the Norman Marcher lords.

Caerphilly 1268

Within little more than a year into the agreement, trouble was already brewing in the Marches of Wales. Many of the castles in the lordship of Brecon which had been ceded over to Llywelyn were still in Norman hands. The Norman Marcher lords found a loophole within the Treaty: the lordship was Llywelyn's by right, but it had never been clarified who owned the castles within it.

Caerphilly Castle, Gilbert De Clare's masterpiece

Llywelyn's pressure for land and revenue encroached on Gilbert De Clare's lordship of Glamorgan in south Wales. The Earl of Gloucester's response was a massive castle building program on the lordships frontier. In 1268 he constructed a castle at Caerphilly, protecting the road to Cardiff and the lowland plains.

Llywelyn attacked the first castle in 1270 and burned it to the ground. The confrontation had become a test of will and power between the Norman Earl and Welsh Prince. Gilbert, who was one of the richest men in England, decided to re-construct the castle at Caerphilly on a grand scale. No expense was spared on the mighty fortress. Caerphilly castle is the largest castle in Wales covering 30 acres and it was also the first concentric castle in Britain. It was so well defended that Llywelyn dared not attack it. King Henry III died in late 1272 and with Prince Edward in the Holy Land on Crusade all control over the Marcher lords evaporated.

The private wars continued in Wales and the Marches until Edward's return in 1274. Llywelyn's position amongst the Welsh nobility was also deteriorating. Unable to defend the Principality from the raids of the Marcher lords, the Welsh conspired behind the Prince's back to overthrow him and replace him with his brother Dafydd. The plot to assassinate Llywelyn was uncovered and the Prince sent his guards to arrest Dafydd and the other conspirators, alas he was too late as the fugitives escaped across the border and took refuge in England.

The sun setting towards Wales from Clun castle

The Reckoning 1274 - 1282

Representatives from Prince Edward arrived at the court of Prince Llywelyn in Wales requesting him to appear before Edward to undertake the obligation of homage, which was required with the accession of a new Monarch. When the royal ambassadors arrived on the English-Welsh border Llywelyn did not show. Edward then sent out an invitation for his coronation, but the Welsh Prince declined the offer and refused to attend. In 1275 the new King travelled to Chester where Llywelyn was ordered to come and renew the oath of fealty. Once again Llywelyn did not turn up; he did however send King Edward a letter explaining that he refused to travel to England where Dafydd and the Welsh rebels were being harboured as he feared for his safety.

The hierarchy of the Kingdom of Britain: King Edward at the top and flanking him on the left King Alexander of Scotland and Prince Llywelyn seated on the right.

Edward's patience was now running out. He had offered the Prince safe conduct and his word he would not be harmed. After waiting several weeks, the King left Chester and headed back to London in a violent rage. Llywelyn received a stark letter instructing him to come to Westminster within a month or face the consequences

The Final Straw

In late 1275 Edward found out that Llywelyn had been secretly negotiating to marry the daughter of his dead arch enemy, Simon de Montfort. Eleanor De Montfort's ship was intercepted on its journey from France to Wales by the King's men. For the King this was virtually a declaration for war. Edward may have wondered if Llywelyn was trying to drum up support with the old diehard De Montfort supporters in England and cause a civil war. His valuable prisoner was sent to the capital and placed under armed

King Edward I of England

guard. In vengence after the discovery of the De Montfort coup d'etat, Edward ordered the Marcher lords to attack Llywelyn's lands at will. The Prince had misjudged his man, for King Edward Plantagenet was to become the most ruthless King to sit on the throne of England.

On the 12th of November 1276 at the King's parliament, Llywelyn "Prince of Wales" was declared an outlaw and disturber of the peace. The King's War council convened and discussed the plan for the forecoming campaign in Wales. During the winter, the Prince sent letters requesting peace, but also with conditions attached to them. The time for negotiating had passed, Llywelyn had opened Pandora's Box and the lion now entered the dragon's lair.

The Invasion of Wales 1277

While the King made the preparations of mustering the royal army, his commanders on the March were tasked with breaking the Welsh resistance along the frontier. In the south, Payn De Chatsworth subdued the southern Welsh nobility into submission. William De Beauchamp (the Earl of Warwick), Henry De Lacy (the Earl of Lincoln) along with Llywelyn's rebellious brother Dafydd advanced into north Wales and besieged the defenders of the ancient hillfort castle of Dinas Bran.

In the middle March Roger De Mortimer raided deep into Montgomeryshire along the Clun valley from his base at Wigmore castle. His objective was the Prince's castle of Dolforwyn.

By the onset of summer 1277 the castles of both Dinas Bran and Dolforwyn had surrendered to the Anglo-Normans. Llywelyn's united Wales had fallen within a few months of the campaign; the Welsh nobles were disappearing from his court and changing sides at an alarming rate. In Worcester the King's younger brother, Edmund, was given command of the reserve forces that were tasked with strangling off Gwynedd from any help from the south. The King mustered his forces at Chester, Edward's army was the largest raised by an English King since the Norman invasion. Over 1000 armoured Knights and up to 15,000 infantry marched into Wales that summer. His strategy was very different to that of his predecessors. As the Norman war machine marched along the north Wales coastline it cleared and cut down the trees and bushes in its path, building a wide road through the densely wooded valleys that had been the defeat of so many armies before it.

The King's men also constructed network of new castles to act as safe havens for his men and break the spirit of Llywelyn's Welsh. The new castles were founded at Flint, Rhuddlan and Aberystwyth. They rose up out of the ground to terrorise the native population into submission. They were built by the sea allowing them to be re-supplied in case they were besieged by the hostile native population.

Rhuddlan castle, in the "Four Cantrefs" modern day Flintshire

The King's fleet sent from the "Cinque Ports" of southern England struck the final hammer blow against Prince Llywelyn. In September they transported 3000 soldiers commanded by Otto De Grandson across the Menai straights onto the island of Anglesey. Within a few days, Otto and the Anglo-Normans had captured the Island, and more importantly, the gain harvest which was vital for Llywelyn. The grain helped maintain Edward's army in the field and forced the Prince who was now surrounded in the "Siege of Snowdon" to surrender.

The Humiliating Peace

In early November 1277, Prince Llywelyn came out of the mist and fog of the Snowdonia Mountains where he had been hiding and surrendered himself to the officials of the King.

The once proud and great man had brought shame and destruction upon himself and Wales by defying the King.

The Prince was forced to accept the humiliating terms of the treaty of Conwy which were harsh but not as harsh as they could have been. Firstly two of the "Four Cantrefs" would remain in English hands; the other two were given to Llywelyn's traitorous brother Dafydd. He then lost his right as overlord over the other Welsh Princes, who now paid homage to King Edward himself. Finally he was fined an enormous sum of over 50,000 marks for damages against the Crown. He was however allowed to keep the empty title of "Prince of Wales" and rule over the remainder of Gwynedd.

Llywelyn was escorted to Rhuddlan castle where he met Edward face to face. The King forgave Llywelyn for his defiance and wavered the 50,000 mark fine, but this was not the end of the matter as far as Edward was concerned. Already humbled by the treaty Llywelyn was to be made an example of. Edward arranged for the Prince to be taken with him back to London to undertake the ceremony of fealty. At Christmas 1277 Llywelyn was paraded through the streets of London and at Westminster before all the nobles of the land he knelt before King Edward I and completed the ritual of homage.

Mathew Paris commented;

"Who does not know that the Prince of Wales is a petit Vassal of the King of England"

Magnanimous in victory, Edward even gave permission and paid for the wedding between Llywelyn and Eleanor De Montfort.

The couple was married in Worcester Cathedral on the 13th of October 1278. As the year ended it seemed that Llywelyn had survived the storm, and averted the total subjugation of his country by the Anglo-Norman King of England.

Worcester, the setting of Prince Llywelyn's marriage in 1278

The Great Rebellion

Apart from Gwynedd which was still directly ruled by Prince Llywelyn, most of Wales was suffering under the oppressive heel of Norman rule. The new Norman lords and administrators exercised contempt towards the native Welsh population who they believed to be inferior to them. Even in the Welsh governed part of the "Four Cantrefs", Dafydd was treated no more than a second class citizen by the Norman officials in Chester. By 1282 the Welsh could take no more and the country exploded in flames.

Hawarden Castle 1282

A secret council of Welsh tribal leaders gathered at Denbigh and declared war against the Normans. The rebellion was scheduled to coincide with the Holy celebrations of Easter. Dafydd launched a daring raid on the Normans at Hawarden castle, close to the English border. The nighttime festivities covered the approach of Dafydd and his Welsh tribesmen.

Then out of the darkness the full fury of the Welsh was unleashed upon the castle. The skillful Welsh bowmen dispatched the sentries while Dafydd's men scaled the walls and overran the castle.
All in the castle were put to the sword and slaughtered; only Roger De Clifford, the Bailli of the castle, was taken hostage.

The remains of Hawarden castle

The Norman Motte and Bailey castle was then ransacked and raised to the ground. Dafydd's act at Hawarden had lit the fire of rebellion that ignited the whole of Wales.

The Rebellion Spreads

Welshmen and women all over the country joined the revolt, attacking the settlements and castles of the Normans. On the west coast Aberystwyth castle fell, in the south Llandovery and the formidable Carreg Cennen fortress also fell into Welsh hands.

The violence was not just restricted to Wales. The great border towns of England including Chester and Oswestry were also attacked. Dafydd laid siege to the symbols of Norman power in the "Four Cantrefs" (the castles of Flint and Rhuddlan).

Prince Llywelyn seems to have had no prior knowledge of the revolt. He was as surprised as the Normans when the news reached his court in Gwynedd. For the time being he refused to join the rebellion; he would wait to see how events unfolded before committing himself. When King Edward heard the news he was extremely disappointed. He became angry and vowed to punish the Welsh for their insolence.

He stated of the Welsh:

"They are a faithless people, their leaders are nothing more than a family of traitors, and it is time to put an end to their malice"

In May 1282 Edward arrived in Worcester. Gilbert De Clare (the Earl of Gloucester) was to take command of the southern forces and quell the rebellion in south Wales. Roger De Mortimer was recalled out of retirement and given the task of stabilising the Middle March. The King meanwhile carried on north to Chester to mobilise the invasion force. As the main army began its assault in north Wales, disastrous news arrived from the south. Gilbert's forces in Carmarthenshire had been wiped out. After retaking the castle of Carreg Cennen, they were ambushed in the wooded valleys of Carmarthenshire. The King's own nephew, William De Valance, lost his life in the debacle.

Edward relieved Gilbert of his command and sent the dead boy's father another William De Valance to avenge his son's death and restore Norman rule in south Wales.

Carreg Cennen Castle, Carmarthenshire Wales

The Last throw of the Dice

Llywelyn who had been sitting on the fence, now made his move. A personal tragedy probably influenced his decision: in June his wife Eleanor De Montfort, who was heavily pregnant, died in childbirth. Their baby survived but it was not a boy as Llywelyn had hoped for. The Prince was by now an old man and Eleanor's death spelt the end of his dreams for the future.

Grief-stricken and now with nothing to lose, Llywelyn threw his lot in with his brother Dafydd and his Welsh countrymen. The final showdown was at hand, where the winner would take it all.

Edward's plan was to capture Anglesey, depriving the Welsh of the important grain reserves, just as he had done in the 1277 campaign. Luc de Tany (the seneschal of Gascony) launched an amphibious assault and secured the Island and the harvest.

The main army of the King advanced towards the river Conwy at a slow pace to avoid being ambushed. William De Valance had subdued the south and retook the coastal town and castle of Aberystwyth. The pincers were now closing in on Snowdonia. Reginald De Grey and the Earl of Surrey marched up the Clwyd valley forcing Dafydd to retreat into the mountains.

The Battle of Moel-y-don

The King planned to construct a pontoon bridge from Anglesey to the mainland which would allow the Normans to attack the Welsh heartland of Snowdonia from two directions. By September the pontoon bridge was complete, but the King's force opposite the river Conwy was not ready to make its attack. By November the impatient Luc De Tany disobeyed the King's orders and decided to launch his attack on Snowdonia alone.

Walter of Guisborough commented:

"The English knights and armed men crossed the bridge at low tide eager for glory and renown."

On the 6th of November 1282 the Anglo Norman knights crossed the pontoon bridge to the mainland. Before the entire army was able to cross, Llywelyn's warriors descended from the mountains and fell upon De Tany's meager force.

"When they had reached the foot of the mountain and, after a time, came to a place at some distance from the bridge, the tide came in with a great flow, so that they were unable to get back to the bridge for the depth of water. The Welsh came from the high mountains and attacked them, and in fear and trepidation, for the great number of the enemy, our men preferred to face the sea than the enemy. They went into the sea but, heavily laden with arms, they were instantly drowned."

Luc De Tany was among the casualties on that fateful day. Sixteen knights were lost and over 300 infantry died on the shores of Snowdonia. The only notable survivor was Otto De Grandson: he tried his luck and swam to the safety of the other side, rather than face capture by the enemy.

The Menai Straight between Anglesey and mainland Snowdonia

The End of Llywelyn the Last, Irfon Bridge 1282

In the same month the old warrior Roger De Mortimer died of natural causes. His death sent the Middle March into chaos. Llywelyn fresh from his victory at the Battle of Moel-y-don, decided the time was right to open up a second front in the Middle March. Leaving Dafydd to hold Snowdonia, Llywelyn headed south to raise rebellion and support for his cause.

On the 11th of December 1282 in the hills near Builth, Llywelyn's force of several thousand Welshmen collided with the Norman Marcher coalition commanded by the Mortimer brothers Edmund and Roger, John Giffard and Roger l'Estrange. It seems that Llywelyn was not with the main army when battle was joined. At Irfon Bridge the Welsh spearmen protected the river crossing and their hilltop position against the Normans. But the Normans were told of a second crossing further downstream. The Norman archers rained countless volleys of deadly arrows onto the tightly packed Welsh Schiltrons, inflicting heavy casualties and depleting their numbers. The slaughter began when the Anglo-Norman cavalry arrived behind the Welsh positions. Now realising they had been outflanked some spearmen panicked and tried to flee, others held their ground and continued to fight to the death. At the end of the day over 3000 Welshmen lay dead on the battlefield.

In the vicinity of Climeri, Llywelyn and a party of knights were ambushed by the Marcher forces. Some say he was returning to the battle, others say he was secretly lured by the Mortimer brothers to discuss the possibility of an alliance. Whatever to truth may be, the Prince was killed in the skirmish by a humble knight Stephen De Frankton. After his body was identified, his head was cut off and sent to King Edward at Rhuddlan castle.

Llywelyn's head was then taken to London where it was paraded through the streets. An ivy crown was placed upon it, as a symbol that Llywelyn was nothing more than a Prince of traitors. It was held high so all the crowd could see what happened to anyone who defied the King, before being displayed on London Bridge for the next 20 years.

Memorial in Welsh to Llywelyn the Last, Cilmery, Wales

"Near this spot was killed our leader Llywelyn 1282"

Dafydd ap Gruffydd 1282-1283

The death of Prince Llywelyn broke the spirit of the Welsh. His brother Dafydd now proclaimed himself Prince of Wales, but his reputation for double dealing and changing sides was never forgotten by his fellow countrymen. Edward's armies swept across Wales eliminating all resistance in its way.

Overleaf the death of Llywelyn the Last, Cilmery, Mid Wales →

Dafydd was a hunted man, fleeing from place to place escaping the clutches of the Anglo-Normans on several occasions. He was finally captured in the summer of 1283 by his fellow countrymen at the foot of Wales's highest mountain (Snowdon).

Royal letters recorded:

"Dafydd ap Gruffydd, last of a treacherous line has been captured, he was handed over by men of his own tongue"

This was the end for the native Princes of Wales, Llywelyn had fallen in battle, but a more gruesome spectacle awaited Dafydd in England. He was taken under armed guard across the border to Shrewsbury. In a showcase trial he was condemned to death for treason.

Arms of Dafydd ap Gruffydd

Firstly he was tied to the tail of a horse and dragged through the streets towards his place of execution.

He was then hanged by the neck, disemboweled and had his entrails burned in front of his eyes, no doubt to the jeers and jubilation of the watching crowd. Finally he was beheaded and quartered. His head was sent to London to rest beside Llywelyn's, the rest of his body parts were distributed to the far flung corners of the Kingdom as a warning to the fate of any would-be traitors.

The Iron Ring

To complete to conquest of Wales, Edward put into motion "The Ring of Iron", a shock and awe policy of castle building on a monumental scale. The castles of Conwy, Caernarfon, Harlech and finally Beaumaris were designed and constructed by the greatest military architect of the time (Master James of St George). The new castles towered over and dominated the defeated Welsh. Caernarfon was built according to an ancient Welsh legend. It was the place, where Magnus Maximus (the father of Constantine, Romes first Christian Emperor) had been buried. When his bones were dug up in 1283, Edward drew upon the symbolism, and commissioned the castle towers to be polygonal instead of cylindrical, copying walls of Constantinople. The finished result is probably the finest medieval castle in Europe.

Caernarfon Castle, North Wales

There were further uprisings in 1287 and more seriously in 1294. The King and his retinue were forced to take refuge in the mighty castle of Conway which was besieged by Madog ap Llywelyn. By 1295 the last rebellion against the Normans had been put down with the defeat of Madog at the Battle of Maes Moydog.

Legend has it that Edward placated the Welsh by promising them a Prince born in Wales that could speak no English. Tradition has it that the prophesy was fore filled when Queen Eleanor gave birth to the future Edward II at Caernafron castle. Edward placed the baby on his shield and presented him to the people of Wales.

Conwy/Conway castle, North Wales

Conclusion

It had taken the Normans 200 years to complete the conquest of Celtic Wales, and was by far the most difficult campaign they had ever undertaken.

The conquest did not mean the end of Wales, or its proud people. The Normans were only interested in the lowland and fertile valleys of the Principality. In the mountains and upland regions the Welsh were left in relative peace and harmony. Their language continued to survive and flourishes to this day. Llywelyn the Last is ultimately responsible for the downfall of his Kingdom by defying England's most ruthless warrior King Edward I. In time the wounds of conquest healed. After the last great revolt by Owain Glyndwr in the 15th century the Welsh wars were finally over.

Edward had also gained a secret weapon from his wars in Wales. The Welsh longbow would be used to defeat the Scots of William Wallace (Braveheart) and Robert the Bruce. It also allowed the Kings of England to regain the Duchy of Normandy, and inflict crushing defeats against the French in the 100 hundred years war.

The Norman hunger for more land and conquest did not stop at the shores of Wales. Across the sea lay the Island of Eire. On the very edge of the known world, the Normans embarked on the conquest of Gallic Ireland. The Irish struggle for liberty against the Anglo-Normans would leave a scare that is only just starting to heal after 750 years of bitter oppression.

Next in the series;

"The Grey Foreigners"

The Norman Conquest of Celtic Ireland

Titles in the series

"THE LAST WAR"

Richard the Lionheart

"THE FIRST MAFIA"

The Norman conquest of
Southern Italy and Sicily

"THE NORMAN CRUSADE"

The First Crusade and the
conquest of the
Kingdom of Heaven

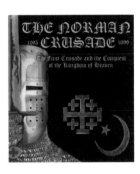

"DOMESDAY 1066"

The Norman conquest
and destruction of
Anglo-Saxon England

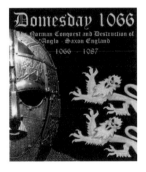

Printed in Great Britain
by Amazon.co.uk, Ltd.,
Marston Gate.